First World War
and Army of Occupation
War Diary
France, Belgium and Germany

30 DIVISION
90 Infantry Brigade
London Regiment
2/16 Battalion (Queen's Westminster Rifles)
1 June 1918 - 31 October 1919

WO95/2340/4

The Naval & Military Press Ltd
www.nmarchive.com
Published in association with The National Archives

Published by

The Naval & Military Press Ltd

Unit 10 Ridgewood Industrial Park,

Uckfield, East Sussex,

TN22 5QE England

Tel: +44 (0) 1825 749494

www.naval-military-press.com

www.nmarchive.com

This diary has been reprinted in facsimile from the original. Any imperfections are inevitably reproduced and the quality may fall short of modern type and cartographic standards.

© **Crown Copyright**
Images reproduced by permission of The National Archives, London, England, 2015.

Contents

Document type	Place/Title	Date From	Date To
Heading	WO95/2340 2/16 London (Queens Westminister Rifles) Jan 18-Oct 19		
Heading	30th Division 90th Infy Bde. 2-16th London Regt. Queen's Westminster Rifles Jun 1918-Oct 1919		
Miscellaneous	Subject. 2/16th London Regt.	00/06/1918	00/06/1918
Heading	2/16th Battn. London Regiment (Queens Westminster Rifles) War Diary June 1st to 30th		
War Diary	Udd Kantara	01/06/1918	30/06/1918
Miscellaneous	War Diary. 2/16th London Regt. Appendix A	00/06/1918	00/06/1918
Miscellaneous	War Diary. 2/16th London Regt. Appendix B	00/06/1918	00/06/1918
Heading	War Diary of the 2/16th London Regt (Queen's Westminster Rifles) for the month of July 1918 Volume No II		
War Diary	Be. F. France	01/07/1918	31/07/1918
Miscellaneous	2/16th London Regt. Appendix	00/07/1918	00/07/1918
Miscellaneous	Subject. 2/16th London Regt.	00/08/1918	00/08/1918
Heading	War Diary Of the 2/16 Battn. Lon. Regt. (Queens Westminster Rifles.) for month of August 1918 Vol 3		
War Diary	In the Field B.E.F.	01/08/1918	31/08/1918
Miscellaneous	2/16th London Regt. War Diary Appendix "A"	00/08/1918	00/08/1918
Miscellaneous	Subject. 2/16th London Regt.	00/09/1918	00/09/1918
Heading	War Diary of 2/16th London Regt Queens Westminster Rifles. Vol 4		
War Diary	In the field France.	01/09/1918	30/09/1918
Miscellaneous	2/16th London Regt. (Q.W.R) War Diary Sept. 1918 Appendix "A"	00/09/1918	00/09/1918
Miscellaneous	Subject. 2/16th London Regt.	00/10/1918	00/10/1918
Heading	War Diary of the 2/16th Bn. London Regt for month of October 1918 Vol 5		
War Diary	Field.	01/10/1918	31/10/1918
War Diary	Field	24/10/1918	25/10/1918
Miscellaneous	2/16th London Regt. War Diary October 1918 Appendix 'A'	00/10/1918	00/10/1918
Miscellaneous	Subject. 2/16th London Regt.	00/11/1918	00/11/1918
Heading	War Diary of 2/16th London Regt. (Queen's Westminster Rifles) Volume no 29		
Miscellaneous	Evidence and Charge Sheets if necessary to be Pinned here.		
War Diary	Field	01/11/1918	30/11/1918
Miscellaneous	2/16th London Regt. War Diary November 1918 Appendix A	00/11/1918	00/11/1918
Miscellaneous	Subject. 2/16th London Regt.	00/12/1918	00/12/1918
Heading	War Diary of 2/16th London Regt. Queens Westminster Rifles Volume no 30		
War Diary	In the Field.	01/12/1918	31/12/1918
Miscellaneous	2/16th London Regiment (Q.W.R.) War Diary, December, 1918. Appendix A.	00/12/1918	00/12/1918
War Diary	Steenbecque.	01/01/1919	31/01/1919
Miscellaneous	2/16th London Regiment. (Q.W.R.) War Diary. Appendix A.	00/01/1919	00/01/1919

War Diary	Calais.	01/02/1919	28/02/1919
Miscellaneous	2/16th London Regiment. (Q.W.R.) War Diary. Appendix A.	00/02/1919	00/02/1919
Heading	War Diary of 2/16th Bn London Regt for February 1919		
War Diary	Calais.	01/03/1919	31/03/1919
War Diary	Calais.	25/03/1919	31/03/1919
Miscellaneous	2/16th London Regiment. (Q.W.R.) War Diary Appendix A.	00/03/1919	00/03/1919
Heading	War Diary of 2/16th London Regt. for March 1919		
War Diary	Calais	01/04/1919	30/04/1919
War Diary	Calais	23/04/1919	30/04/1919
War Diary	Calais	26/04/1919	30/04/1919
Miscellaneous	2/16th London Regiment (Q.W.R.) War Diary Appendix A.	00/04/1919	00/04/1919
Heading	War Diary of 2/16th London Regt for April 1919		
Heading	War Diary Of The 2/16th London Regiment (Queen's Westminster Rifles.) For The Month Of May 1919. Vol 12		
War Diary	Calais	01/05/1919	28/05/1919
War Diary	Calais	01/05/1919	31/05/1919
Miscellaneous	2/16th London Regiment. (Queen's Westminster Rifles.) War Diary Appendix 'A'	00/05/1919	00/05/1919
Heading	War Diary Of 2/16th London Regiment. (Queens) Westminster Rifles) For The Month Of June, 1919 Volume No 36		
War Diary	Abbeville.	04/06/1919	23/06/1919
War Diary	Abbeville.	01/06/1919	30/06/1919
Miscellaneous	2/16th London Regiment (Queen's Westminster Rifles.) War Diary Appendix 'A'	00/06/1919	00/06/1919
Heading	War Diary Of 2/16th London Regiment (Queen's Westminster Rifles.) For The Month Of July 1919 Vol No 36		
War Diary	Abbeville.	01/07/1919	31/07/1919
War Diary	Abbeville.	22/07/1919	31/07/1919
War Diary	Abbeville.	01/07/1919	31/07/1919
Miscellaneous	2/16th London Regiment (Queen's Westminster Rifles.) War Diary Appendix A.	00/07/1919	00/07/1919
Heading	War Diary Of 2/16th Battalion The London Regiment. (Queen's Westminster Rifles.) For The Month Of August 1919 Vol No. 37		
War Diary	Abbeville.	01/08/1919	31/08/1919
War Diary	Abbeville.	15/08/1919	31/08/1919
War Diary	Abbeville.	01/08/1919	31/08/1919
Miscellaneous	2/16th London Regiment (Queen's Westminster Rifles.) War Diary Appendix A.	00/08/1919	00/08/1919
Heading	War Diary Of 2/16th London Regiment (Queen's Westminster Rifles.) For The Month Of September 1919. (Volume No. 38.)		
War Diary	Abbeville	01/09/1919	30/09/1919
War Diary	Abbeville	01/09/1919	25/09/1919
War Diary	Abbeville	01/09/1919	24/09/1919
War Diary	Abbeville	01/09/1919	23/09/1919
War Diary	Abbeville	01/09/1919	24/09/1919
War Diary	Abbeville	01/09/1919	21/09/1919

Miscellaneous	2/16th London Regiment (Queen's Westminster Rifles) War Diary Appendix 'A" September 1919	00/09/1919	00/09/1919
Heading	War Diary Of 2/16th London Regiment (Queen's Westminster Rifles.) for the month of October 1919 Volume No 39		
Miscellaneous	Cover for Documents. Nature of Enclosures.		
War Diary	Abbeville	01/10/1919	31/10/1919
Miscellaneous	2/16th London Regiment (Queen's Westminster Rifles.) War Diary Appendix 'A" October 1919	00/10/1919	00/10/1919

WO 95/2340
2/16 London
(Queens Westminster Rifles)
June '18 – Oct '19

30TH DIVISION
90TH INFY BDE

WO95-2340

2-16TH LONDON REGT.
(QUEEN'S WESTMINSTER RIFLES)
JUN 1918-OCT 1919

FROM "FGYH"
60 DIV 179 BDE

B. 2340

Index...........................

90/30

SUBJECT.

2/16th London Regt.

No.	Contents.	Date.
	June 1918.	

2/16TH BATTN. LONDON REGIMENT
(QUEENS WESTMINSTER RIFLES)

WAR

DIARY

JUNE 1st to 30TH.

Army Form C. 2118.

WAR DIARY
2/16th BATTN. LONDON (QUEEN'S WESTMINSTER RIFLES)
or
INTELLIGENCE SUMMARY.
(Erase heading not required.)

Instructions regarding War Diaries and Intelligence Summaries are contained in F. S. Regs., Part II. and the Staff Manual respectively. Title pages will be prepared in manuscript.

Place	Date	Hour	Summary of Events and Information	Remarks and references to Appendices
LUDD	June 1	4 pm	Batt. entrained LUDD	PALESTINE
KANTARA	" 2	9.30 am	" detrained at KANTARA	
	" 3 to June 14		Batt. at KANTARA. Company & Specialist training — awaiting embarkation.	Appendix A
	June 15		Entrained Kantara	Batty attestation in Strength
	" 16		Detrained ALEXANDRIA and embarked on H.M.T. "INDARRA"	
	" 18		Sailed	
	" 21	11.0 am	H.M.T. "INDARRA" unsuccessfully attacked by submarine in Gulf of Taranto. Lt. Col. J.H. YOUNG M.C. commdg. troops abroad	Appendix "B" Nominal roll of Officers proceeding overseas with Unit.
	" 22	2 pm	Arrived outer harbour TARANTO	
	" 23	7 am	Disembarked TARANTO	
	" 24		Batt. in Camp TARANTO	
	" 26	11 pm	Batt. entrained TARANTO	
	" 27			
	" 28		Batt. in train en route for France.	
	" 29			
	" 30			

J.H. Young LT. COL.
COMDG. 2/16TH BATTALION LONDON REGIMENT.
(QUEEN'S WESTMINSTER RIFLES.)

WAR DIARY 2/16TH LONDON REGT.

APPENDIX A   June 1918

Date	Off's	OR	Changes
1-6-18	28	604	2nd Lieut W.H. Crick (draft) and 39 ORs from Hospital. 2 OR's to Hospital
2-6-18	29	641	2 OR's to Hospital
3-6-18	29	639	1 Off + 29 ORs Advance party to France. Lt. Inst Brakspear from Detachment
4-6-18	29	610	Capt Archibold, 2/Lt H. McKay, 2/Lt J.S. Reeve from Hospital, 2nd Lt Lowe (draft) 49 OR's from Hospital
5-6-18	33	659	Capt T.J. Bruce from Hospital. Lieut NH Hart from Detachment
6-6-18	35	659	1 OR transferred to 2/13th Lond R.
7-6-18	35	658	38 OR's from Hospital + 6 OR's from Detachment
8-6-18	35	702	1 OR from Trade Test + 4 OR's from Courses
9-6-18	35	707	Capt R.C. Dalton, Lt P.C. Giannacopulo, 2nd Lt W.C. Jordan, Lieut C Wenren, 2nd Lt T.S. White + 37 OR's from Hospital
10-6-18	40	744	2 OR's from Hospital + 2 OR's from Detachment
11-6-18	40	748	1 OR from Hospital
12-6-18	40	749	No change
13-6-18	40	749	10 OR's from Hospital
14-6-18	40	759	1 Off (Lt Col J.H. Young) 10 OR's from Hosp
15-6-18	41	759	Capt Stanham, Capt R.C. Dalton M.C., Lt W. Brakspear, Lt C Wenren, Lt N.N. Hart, 2nd Lt Satchell, 2nd Lt Mills, 2nd Lt Jordan, 2nd Lt Nhuvakey, 2nd Lt Crick, 2nd Lt Trapaud, 2nd Lt Lowe and 16 OR's left behind in Egypt on Unit proceeding overseas. Lt. S. Gibbon from Detachment 2/6/18.
16-6-18	30	753	Batln Embarked for Overseas
17-6-18	30	753	1 OR to Hosp. from Ship.
18-6-18	30	752	
24-6-18	30	752	4 OR's to Hospital
25-6-18	30	748	6 OR's to Hospital
26-6-18	30	742	3 OR's to Hospital
28-6-18	30	739	No change
29-6-18	30	739	No change
30-6-18	30	739	No change

J.H. Young
LT. COL.
COMG 2/16TH BATTALION LONDON REGIMENT.
(QUEEN'S WESTMINSTER RIFLES.)

WAR DIARY   2/16th LONDON REGT

APPENDIX B   June 1918

Nominal Roll of Officers proceeded with Unit
overseas
───────────────────────────

Lt Col   J. H. Young M C
Capt (a/Major) C. H. Flower M C
Lieut (a/Capt) W. W. Bruce
      "   T. J. Bruce M C
      "   E. P. Gibbins
      "   P. G. Giannacopulo
      (a/Capt) W. Mortimer
      "   A. Archibold
      "   R. N. Bates
      "   K. Frazer
      "   F. B. Leite
      "   E. C. Taylor
  2nd Lieut   R. G. Shuter
      "   H. G. McKay
      "   J. F. Boyes
      "   J. S. Reeve
      "   J. J. Best
      "   S. J. Kinsey
      "   F. J. West
      "   T. S. White
      "   G. S. Mason
      "   R. C. Pierpoint
      (a/Capt) J. W. Chinnin M C
      "   G. B. Morris
      "   T. H. Smith
      "   W. S. Haynes
      "   G. Griffith
      "   J. W. Scott

Capt + Adjt. J. Bowman Vaughan
Hon Capt & QM C. J. Trollope
Capt   G. L. Thornton M C (R.A.M.C.) attd

                            J. H. Young LT. COL.
                   COMG. 2/16TH BATTALION LONDON REGIMENT.
                        (QUEEN'S WESTMINSTER RIFLES.)

Secret Volume No. II

War Diary
of the
2/16th London Regt (Queen's Westminster Rifles)
for the month of July, 1918.

In the field
4th Aug. 1918

C. L. Forster, Major
Commanding 2/16th London Regt

2/16th BATTN. LONDON REGT.
(QUEEN'S WESTMINSTER RIFLES)

Army Form C. 2118.

WAR DIARY
or
INTELLIGENCE SUMMARY.
(Erase heading not required.)

Instructions regarding War Diaries and Intelligence Summaries are contained in F. S. Regs., Part II. and the Staff Manual respectively. Title pages will be prepared in manuscript.

JULY 1918.

Place	Date	Hour	Summary of Events and Information	Remarks and references to Appendices
B.E.F. France	July 1918. 1st		Battn. detrained at AUDRUICQ and marched to billets in vicinity of MOULLE	HAZEBROUCK 1/10,000
	2nd to 7th		Battn. at MOULLE undergoing training. Battn. reorganized in accordance with war establishments during this period. Battn. joined 90: Inf. Bde., forming part of 30 Div.	
	8th		Battn. marched in Bde. to FORT ROUGE near RENESCURE	
	9th		" " " " ST SYLVESTRE CAPPEL	
	10th to 16th		Battn. in training at ST. SYLVESTRE CAPPEL. Platoon + company training. Battn. inspected by B.O.C. 2nd Army on morning of 13th.	
	17th	1 p.m.	Battn. moved out from billets and took up Battle Stations in vicinity of BOESCHEPE returning to billets at 10 a.m. on 18th	
	19th to 20th		Battn. in training at ST SYLVESTRE CAPPEL including a Bde Demonstration on 22nd and an aeroplane demonstration on 24th.	
	25th		Battn. moved to MUTH FARM, R.8.C. 9.5 + relieved the 12 H.L.I (in reserve to 106 Bde)	BERTHEN 10,000
	26th		Battn. moved into Support of 2/15 London Regt. in vicinity of MONT VIDAIGNE.	WESTOUTRE 10,000
	27th to 31st		Battn. in Support about MONT VIDAIGNE 19.21. 31 OR. sent to Armentières as Divl. Reinforcements. (2/15: in front line. 2/14 in Bde reserve).	SCHERPENBERG 10,000

J W Martin
Capt & for Major
Comdg 2/16 London Regt.

WAR DIARY
2/16TH LONDON REGT.
APPENDIX " "

DATE	O/S	OR	CHANGES.
1-7-18	30	739	+ 1 officer (Lieut R.N.Bates) and 29 OR's advance party from Egypt - 6 OR's to Hospital.
2-7-18	31	762	
3-7-18	31	762	1 OR from Hospital
4-7-18	31	761	4 OR's to Hospital
5-7-18	31	757	1 OR from Hospital
7-7-18	31	758	4 OR's to Hospital, 1 OR from Hospital
8-7-18	31	755	1 officer (2nd Lt Smith) & 2 OR's to Hospital
10-7-18	30	753	5 OR's to Hospital
11-7-18	30	748	2 OR's to Hospital
12-7-18	30	746	1 OR from Hospital
14-7-18	30	747	1 OR from Hospital
15-7-18	30	748	31 OR's draft + 3 officers (draft) (2nd Lt Stevens, 2nd Lt Wiltshire, 2nd Lt Payne) 1 officer from Hospital (2nd Lt Smith) 1 OR from Hospital
17-7-18	34	780	
18-7-18	34	780	5 OR's to Base unfit
19-7-18	34	775	2 OR's from Hospital
20-7-18	34	777	5 OR's to Hospital
22-7-18	34	772	1 OR to Cadet School England
23/7/18	34	771	151 OR's draft + 1 OR to Cadet School England.
24/7/18	34	921	10 OR's draft + 1 OR from Hospital
25-7-18	34	932	1 OR from Hospital
26-7-18	34	933	
27-7-18	34	933	10 OR's to Hospital
31-7-18	30	923	4 OR to hospital (wounded). 2 OR. to hospital sick. 30/f. 917.

Index..................

SUBJECT.

2/16th London Regt.

No.	Contents.	Date.
	August 1918.	

SECRET VOLUMN No 26.

War Diary
of the
2/16 Battn. Lon. Regt.
(Queens Westminster Rifles.)
for month of
AUGUST
1918.

2.9.18.

C H Flower, Major Lt. Col.
Comdg 2/16 Lon. Regt.

2/16th Battn. LONDON REGT.

WAR DIARY
or
INTELLIGENCE SUMMARY.
(Erase heading not required.)

Army Form C. 2118.

August 1918.

Place	Date	Hour	Summary of Events and Information	Remarks and references to Appendices
On the Dues BER	AUG 1st		Battn. moved to front line in LOCRE Sector relieving 2/14 London Regt.	78. S.W.1.
do.	2nd		Battn. holding line in above Sector.	do.
do.	3rd		" relieved in front line by 15th Bn Sherwood Foresters & moved into 90th Bde Reserve about MOTH FARM (R.8.c.8.5)	do.
do.	4th		90th Inf. Bde., including this Battn. moved to Rest Billets in ST. SYLVESTRE CAPPEL	27. S.E. Eastern Half HAZEBROOK 5A
do.	5th 6th 7th 8th		Battn. in training at ST. SYLVESTRE CAPPEL	do.
do.	9th 10th		Battn. moved to MOTH FARM (R.8.c.8.5)	27. S.E. Eastern Half
do.	16th		Battn. in training at MOTH FARM.	do.
do.	17th		Battn. relieved 2/14 Lond. R. about M.23.a.6.4 and became 2/15th Lond. R. in LOCRE H.O.F. Sector Sub	28. S.W.1.
do.	18th		Battn. relieved 2/15 " in front line of LOCREHOF Subsector.	do.
do.	19		Battn. holding front line positions	do.
do.	20		Battn. relieved by 4th L.R. who advanced to a depth of 1000 yds. D. Coy 2/16 forming carrying party to 2/14 d. B. Coy 2/16 occupying the BLUE LINE about M.28.a.6.5 in close support Remainder of Battn. in Bde. support about M.22.a.4.5.	do.
do.	21		B. Coy 2/16 on BLUE LINE relieved by C. Coy 2/16"	do.
do.	22.		Battn. relieved by 2/14 Lond. R. and moved back into 90 Bde Reserve at MOTH FARM (R.8.c.8.5)	27. S.E. Eastern Half

(2).

WAR DIARY
or
INTELLIGENCE SUMMARY.
(Erase heading not required.)

Army Form C. 2118.

AUG. 1918.

Place	Date	Hour	Summary of Events and Information	Remarks and references to Appendices
In the Field B.E.F.	AUG. 23rd		Battn. relieved by 2/17. Battn. in reserve of 90' Bde at MOTH FARM	27. S.E. Eastern Ho.15
do	24th		Battn. moved into support of 2/16 in LOCREHOF Sub-sector. A. Coy. holding BLUE LINE	28. S.W.1.
do	25th		Battn. in support to 2/15th Lond.R.	do.
do	26th		Battn. moved to front line positions in same sector relieving 2/15 Lond.R.	do.
do	27th 29		Battn. holding line.	do.
do	30		Battn. advance to to a depth of about 1200 yds.	do.
do	31		Battn. relieved by 6" Cheshire Regt and 17 Bn. London Regt & moved back to former support area about MONT VIDAIGNE (M.21.a.5.4.) taking over from 1/8th INNS. FUS.	do.
				Strength appx. exc. including casualties attack 1.

[signature]
Major Lt. Col.
COMg. 2/18TH BATTALION LONDON REGIMENT.
(QUEEN'S WESTMINSTER RIFLES.)

2/16th LONDON REGT.

WAR DIARY

APPENDIX 'A'

DATE	OFFs	OR's	CHANGES.
1.8.18	33	923	4 OR's wounded & evacuated.
2.8.18	33	919	1 OR to Base unfit, 1 OR wounded & evacuated.
3.8.18	33	917	
5.8.18	33	917	2 OR's from Hospital Egypt, 1 OR wounded, 3 OR's evacuated to C.C.S., 2 officers joined from Base (2nd Lt W. Scott & 2nd Lt F.C. Tickell.
6.8.18	35	915	
7.8.18	35	915	4 OR's rejoined from Hospital
8.8.18	35	919	2 officers joined from Base (2nd Lt E. Gidden & 2nd Lt W.A. Harris.
9.8.18	37	919	
10.8.18	37	919	5 OR's evacuated to C.C.S.
11.8.18	37	914	
12.8.18	37	914	1 OR to Hospital (England)
13.8.18	37	913	2 OR's from Hospital Egypt.
14.8.18	37	915	1 OR from Hospital Egypt.
15.8.18	37	916	1 officer awaiting Medical Board in England (A/Capt P.C. Giannacopulo) 1 OR transferred to R E's
16.8.18	36	915	
19.8.18	36	915	11 OR's draft joined from Base
21.8.18	36	926	12 OR's evacuated to C.C.S. 1 officer wounded (2nd Lt W. Scott) 2 OR's Killed in Action, 9 OR's wounded, 1 officer invalided to England (Capt J.B Vaughan)
22.8.18	34	903	9 OR's from Hospital, 5 OR's from Hospital Egypt. 3 OR's (draft), 1 OR Killed in Action, 4 OR's wounded
23.8.18	34	908	2 officers wounded (2nd Lt J.F. Boyes, Capt A. Archibold) 1 OR killed in Action, 19 OR's wounded, 2nd Lt J.W Scott invalided to England.
24.8.18	31	888	1 OR wounded & evacuated.
25.8.18	31	887	1 OR ,, ,,
26.8.18	31	886	14 OR's draft joined from Base.
27.8.18	31	900	1 O.R. to Base underage, 13 OR's to C.C.S., 1 OR discharged unfit - 1 OR wounded
28.8.18	31	884	1 OR wounded
30.8.18	31	883	
31.8.18	31	883	3 OR's from Hospital Egypt, 1 OR from Hospital, 5 OR's wounded, 10 OR's draft from Base, 9 OR's from Hospital Egypt. 2 officers from Base (2nd Lt S.J. Holcombe and 2nd Lieut G. Rankin.

Index..........................

SUBJECT.

2/16th London Regt.

90/30

No.	Contents.	Date.
	September 1918.	

Secret

Volume No. 27.

War Diary
- of -
2/16th London Regt.
Queen's Westminster Rifles.

Sept. 1918.

W.J. Pearson
Lt. Col.
Commdg: 2/16th London Regt.

2/16th Bn. LONDON REGT (QUEEN'S WESTMINSTER RIFLES).

WAR DIARY
or
INTELLIGENCE SUMMARY.
(Erase heading not required.)

Army Form C. 2118.

SEPTEMBER 1918.

Place	Date	Hour	Summary of Events and Information	Remarks and references to Appendices
On the field France.	Sept. 1st		Battn. in reserve to 30th Austrian Divn. at MONT KEMMEL (M.21.a.5.4)	Sheet 28 Belgium & Part of France
	2nd		Battn. moved forward to reserve of 90. Bde. in vicinity of M.36.	do.
	3rd		Moved to support of 2/15th Lond. R. in line about M.35.d.5.3. Bn. HQ. at T.3.b.3.4	do.
	4th		Bn. in support to 2/15 Lond. R.	do.
	5th		Battn. took over line from 2/15 Lond. R.	do.
	6th		Battn. holding line. Patrols etc.	do.
	7th		do. do. do.	do.
	8th		90 Bde. relieved by 89th Bde. 2/16th moved back to M.34.d	do.
	9th		90 Bde. to Div Reserve – 2/16th to MONT ROUGE (M.22.a.5.4)	do.
	10th 11th 18th		Battn. in training at MONT ROUGE	do.
	19th		Battn. relieved 2/14th at ULSTER CAMP. (M.35.c.8.2) & became support to 21st Bde.	do.
	20th		Battn. moved into reserve of 90 Bde at BAILLEUL ASYLUM (S.8.d.7.3)	do.
	21st 24th		Battn. at BAILLEUL ASYLUM undergoing training	do.
	25th		Battn. relieved 2/14th in line in vicinity of WULVERGHEM. 3 Coys in line, 1 in Battn. reserve	do.
	26th		Battn in line - 2 Coys relieved by 114th East Rancs. and joined Battn. reserve.	do.
	27th		Battn. in line - one Coy. front. (B. Coy).	do.

Army Form C. 2118.

WAR DIARY
or
INTELLIGENCE SUMMARY.
(Erase heading not required.)

SEPTEMBER 1918.

Place	Date	Hour	Summary of Events and Information	Remarks and references to Appendices
In the Field France	Sept. 28th		90th Bde. ordered to advance - Final objective being a line running N & S. about 1500 yds. E. of MESSINES.	Sheet 28. BELGIUM & part of France.
		0530	2/15th Lond. R. sent forward fighting patrols under cover of artillery M.G. & T.M. barrage. 2/16 remaining in same position.	do
		3 pm.	2/16th Lond. R. attacked and took first objective about U.I.d, U.2.c, U.7.b.d. U.8. & 1.c. These objective were held night. 28/29th.	do
	29th.		90 Bde ordered to advance to COMINES Canal. 2/16th, with 2/15d on left, advanced and reached this objective by 14.30 hs. Battn. remained the night in vicinity of P.19. d.o.5 with 2. Coys on COMINES Canal	do do do
	30th		2/14th Lond. R. took over line and Battn withdrew to Bde. reserve about T.6.	do. do
				Strength & Appendices attached

Signed [signature]
LT. COL.
Queen's Westminster Rifles
(D)

2/16th LONDON REGT. (Q.W.R.)

WAR DIARY. Sept. 1918

Appendix "A"

Date.	Off	O.R.	Changes.
1.9.18	33	902	
2.9.18	33	902	Lt. Col. PEARSON taken on strength also batman, 1 O.R. to hosp.
3.9.18	34	902	1 O.R. to hosp. wounded, 2 O.R. from Base.
4.9.18	34	903	
5.9.18	34	903	2 O.R. wounded
6.9.18	34	901	2 O.R. wounded.
7.9.18	34	899	2 O.R. K.in.A. 2/Lt. C.H. STEVENS, 2/Lt. J.F. PAYNE & 12 O.R. wounded 2 O.R. from hospital, 1 O.R. to hospital sick
8.9.18	32	886	8 O.R. wounded
9.9.18	32	878	16 O.R. from Base, 38 O.R. evacuated sick & struck off.
10.9.18	32	856	1 O.R. K.in.A. 12 O.R. wounded, 1 O.R. evacuated sick, 2 O.R. from hosp.
11.9.18	32	844	3 O.R. from hosp. 2 O.R. evacuated sick
12.9.18	32	845	2nd Lt. F.A. READ, M.A. from overseas
13.9.18	33	845	4 O.R. from hospital.
14.9.18	33	849	21 O.R. from Base
15.9.18	33	870	Capt. H.D. CORLETT, Lieut. S.E. TROTTER, 2/Lt. A.W. PICKWORTH, 2/Lt. G.H. MOTTRAM 2/Lt. J.M. BERNARD, 2/Lt. J.R. POPE & 3 O.R. from Base, 25 O.R. evacuated sick
16.9.18	39	848	5 O.R. from hosp. 1 O.R. to R.A.F. 3 N.C.Os to U.K. for exchange
17.9.18	39	849	2/Lt. H.W. SUMSION, 2/Lt. C.D. SMITH D.C.M. M/Lt. W.L. PRATT & 1 O.R. from Base
18.9.18	42	850	2 O.R. to 90 T.M. By.
19.9.18	42	848	6 O.R. from hosp. 3 O.R. to Base unfit, 1 N.C.O. to U.K. for exchange.
20.9.18	42	850	1 O.R. to U.K. commission. 1 O.R. to U.K. R.A.F. & 2 N.C.Os for exchange
21.9.18	42	846	4 O.R. from Base
22.9.18	42	850	
23.9.18	42	850	1 O.R. to U.K commission
24.9.18	42	849	10 O.R. evacuated sick
25.9.18	42	839	1 O.R. to U.K. commission
26.9.18	42	838	10 O.R. from Base
27.9.18	42	848	1 O.R. wounded 3 O.R. from hosp.
28.9.18	42	850	1 O.R. evacuated sick
29.9.18	42	849	3 " "
30.9.18	42	846	Capt. K. ELMES (R.A.M.C. attd.) K.in A. 2/Lt. A.W. PICKWORTH K.in A. 16 O.R. killed in action. 2/Lt. W.G. HAYNES, 2/Lt. G.H. MOTTRAM, Capt. H.D. CORLETT 2/Lt E. GIDDEN, Lieut. F.B. LEETE & 79 O.R. wounded. (Casualties took place on 28th & 29th).

Total. 36. 751

Index..................

SUBJECT.

2/16-th London Regt.

No.	Contents.	Date.
	October 1918.	

Secret   Vol. No. 28.

War Diary
of the
2/16th Bn. London Regt

for month of October, 1918.

4.11.18.

W. Pearson Lt. Col.
Comdg. 2/16th London Regt.

2/16 Bn London Regt., Queens Westminster Rifles.

Army Form C. 2118.

WAR DIARY
or
INTELLIGENCE SUMMARY.
(Erase heading not required.)

October 1918

Place	Date	Hour	Summary of Events and Information	Remarks and references to Appendices
Field	Oct. 1st–5th		Bn. in reserve. Bn. at JOYE FARM O.22.d.7.2. Training & making roads in good order. Rem. H.Q. & Tpt. Lines at N.28.c.9.7.	CWF Sheet 28 1/40000
	6th		Bn. moved to RENTY FARM O.13.b.9.5. Bn. still in reserve.	CWF "
	11th		Training & considerable amount of german aircraft were active in his area.	CWF "
	9th		Rear H.Q. & Tpt. Lines moved to O.15.c.7.5	CWF "
	12th		Bn. moved to vicinity of HOUTHEM and after dark relieved 2/17th Lon. R. at TENBRIELEN P.22.b.9.3 and became Support to 2/14 & 2/15th Bn. Lon. R. who were holding line.	CWF "
	13th		Bn. at TENBRIELEN in Support.	CWF "
	14th		9.0 F. Bdi. attacked with 2/st Bde on R. and 34th Div. on L. 2/14 & 2/15th Bn. Lon R in line.	CWF "
	15th	15th	2/16th Bn. in Support at TENBRIELEN. WERVICQ aflamed.	CWF "
	15th		Bn. in Support at TENBRIELEN	CWF "
	16th		Bn. moved into line on L. of 2/14. relieving 2/7th HEREFORDS (34th Div.) Bn. H.Q. at Q.18.b.20.50 Line conformed to course of R. LYS. Patrols crossed river during night by means of rafts. Rear H.Q. & Tpt. line moved to P.10.d.8.6.	CWF "
	17th		Bn. crossed R. LYS and advanced through BOUSBECQUE and HALLUIN and took up an outpost position N.E. of HALLUIN. Bn. H.Q. at TRIEZ CAILLOUX R.33.b.3.4	CWF "

2/16th LONDON REG. QUEEN'S WESTMINSTER RIFLES.

WAR DIARY
or
INTELLIGENCE SUMMARY.
(Erase heading not required.)

Army Form C. 2118.

OCTOBER 1918.

Place	Date	Hour	Summary of Events and Information	Remarks and references to Appendices
FIELD	17th		Rear HQ & Tpt crossed LYS at BOUSBECQUE during night 17/18th and joined off	Sheet 28
	18th		Bn at TRIER CAILLOUX early on the 18th.	off 1/40,000
			Bn advanced through DRONKAARD and gained touch with enemy E. off	
			Railway in M.27.b. Bn attacked during night 18/19th but was only off	Sheet 29 1/40,000
			partially successful owing to hostile M.G. fire. Arrangements were made for off	
			a further attack at dawn but enemy withdrew before this hour.	"
	19th		Bde still Advance Guard to Div. advance continued with 2/16th on L and off	"
			2/14th on R. of Bde front. At dusk Bn had reached line T.2.6 85.35 along off	"
			road through T.3.c., T.9.a. and T.9.c. b first in front of Fre HERBAU. off	"
			During night patrol felt their way forward to main road in T.5.6, T.5.d, T.11.b off	"
			T.11.d and before dawn posts were to establish had at T.5.d 4.9. T.11.b 6.1. off	"
			and T.17.a. 6.6. and linked attained with units on R. and L.	"
	20th		Posns on above were handed over to 2/0 Bde about 0900 hrs and Bn off	"
			was collected into billets with Bn H.Q at KWADEBRUG. Bde became off	"
			Div. Reserve.	"
	21st		Bn moved into billets in farms N. of DOTTIGNIES. Bn H.Q at off	"

2/16 LONDON REG. QUEEN'S WESTMINSTER R.F.E.S.

Army Form C. 2118.

WAR DIARY
INTELLIGENCE SUMMARY.

OCTOBER 1918.

(Erase heading not required.)

Place	Date	Hour	Summary of Events and Information	Remarks and references to Appendices
Field.	21st		LIAGRE FARM T.22.a.6.0	off
	22		Bn in Div Reserve Bn at and near LIAGRE FARM. Training. Baths	off Sheet 28 off 1/40000
	23		Disinfecting.	off
	24th		Concert by Bn "Troupe" at DOTTIGNIES concert hall	off
	25th		"Optimists" gave performance for Bn in concert hall in DOTTIGNIES.	off

W Pearson Lt. Col.
comdg. 2/16th Battalion London Regiment
(Queen's Westminster Rifles)

2/16TH LONDON REGT

WAR DIARY   October 1918

APPENDIX 'A'

DATE	OFFS	ORs	CHANGES
1st Oct 1918	36	751	18 OR's evacuated to CCS.
2nd " "	36	733	5 OR's wounded & evacuated.
3rd " "	36	728	1 OR wounded
4th " "	36	727	15 OR's draft from Base & 13 OR's from Hospital
5 " "	36	755	2nd Lieut G.B. MORRIS invalided to England.
6 " "	35	755	18 OR's from Hospital - Base
7 " "	35	773	Lt.Col J.H. YOUNG. M.C. to 1/5th Argyll & Sutherland Highlanders + 1 OR from Hospital.
8 " "	34	774	2 OR's from Hospital - Egypt. and. 2 OR's admitted to Hospital whilst on leave in U.K.
9 " "	34	774	
10 " "	34	774	
11 " "	34	774	
12 " "	34	774	
13 " "	34	774	13 OR's wounded & evacuated, 2 OR's K in A, 2 OR's wounded. 4 OR's rejoined from Hospital
14 " "	34	761	22 OR's evacuated to CCS from Fd Amb. 3 OR's rejoined from Hospital
15 " "	34	772	30 OR's draft from Base, 8 OR's rejoined from Hospital 13 OR's wounded & evacuated.
16 " "	34	767	2 OR's from Base, 2 OR's wounded
17 " "	34	767	
19 " "	34	767	4 OR's K in A, 2nd Lt H.G. McKAY + 5 OR's wounded
20 " "	33	758	7 OR's wounded
21 " "	33	751	3 OR's from Base
22 " "	33	754	
25 " "	33	754	36 draft from Base, 17 OR's rejoined from Hospital 1 OR to R.A.F.
26 " "	33	806	2 OR's to T.M.B., 98 OR's evacuated to C.C.S from Fd Amb. 1 OR from Hospital, 1 OR to Base, 2 OR's died of disease
27 " "	33	704	14 OR's evacuated to CCS + 2 OR's to Base
28 " "	33	688	15 OR's from Hospital - Base. 11 OR's to Hospital
29 " "	33	692	1 OR from Hospital
30 " "	33	693	13 draft from Base, 2 OR's from Hospital 10 OR's evacuated to Hospital
31 " "	33	698	10 OR's draft from Base, 7 OR's evacuated to Hospital.

Total   33 offs   701

Index..............................

SUBJECT.

2/16th London Regt.

No.	Contents.	Date.
	November 1918.	

Secret   Volume No. 29.

War Diary
- of -
2/16th London Regt.
(Queen's Westminster Rifles.)

November 1918.

Major Commanding,
2/16th London Regt.
(Q.W.R.)

Evidence and Charge Sheets (if necessary) to be PINNED here.

3

I certify that the above Court assembled on the day of   , and duly tried the persons named in the Schedule, and that the plea, finding, and sentence in the case of each such person were as stated in the third and fourth columns of that Schedule.

B.
Certificate of President as to proceedings.

I also certify that
1. The members of the Court
2. The witnesses
* (3. The interpreter)
* (4. The officers under instruction)

were duly sworn.

* Omit if not applicable.

Signed this   day of   19   .

_____
President of the Court Martial.

I have dealt with the findings and sentences in the manner stated in the last column of the Schedule, and, subject to what I have there stated, I hereby confirm the above findings and sentences.

C.
Confirmation.

* To be omitted unless penal servitude or imprisonment having been awarded, the Confirming Officer either has no authority to commit to prison, or, having such authority, recommends suspension.

* (I direct that the soldier named in the margin be not committed to prison until further orders.)

Signed this   day of   19   .

_____
Confirming Officer.

Promulgated and extracts taken in the case of

(a) (Dated)_____ (Signed)_____

Promulgated and extracts taken in the case of

(Dated)_____ (Signed)_____

Promulgated and extracts taken in the case of

(Dated)_____ (Signed)_____

(a) When several cases are promulgated in one unit on the same day the Officer need only sign once.

Army Form C. 2118.

WAR DIARY
or
INTELLIGENCE SUMMARY.
(Erase heading not required.)

Instructions regarding War Diaries and Intelligence Summaries are contained in F. S. Regs., Part II. and the Staff Manual respectively. Title pages will be prepared in manuscript.

Place	Date	Hour	Summary of Events and Information	Remarks and references to Appendices
Field	1/11/18		Bt. took over line from 21st Bde. 2/23 London R. and 1 Coy 6E CHESHIRE R. C Coy on right, D Coy on Left. A Coy left support, B Coy right support. Limit of front U.24.b.5.5. to V.9.d.2.0. Bt. A.Q. at U.6.d.3.8. T.H. line at N.29.b.3.5.	Sheet 29 1/40,000
	2/11/18		Night patrol along L. bank of R. SCHELDT. Left flank extended to V.3.d.2.4. A Coy in front line at L 67.	
	3/11/18		C. Coy Patrol a.m. 2/11/18. Relief ordered and cancelled.	
	4/11/18			
	6/11/18		Front extended by A Coy to V.4.a.8.6. One Coy 2/15 Lon. R moved into support under command 7 C.v. 2/16 Lon. R. also 50 O.R. C/15 Cyclist.	
	7/11/18		R. front Coy and R. support Coy relieved by a Bt. of 88th Inf Bde 2/16 Lon. R. came under orders of 89 Bde. C Coy relieved by 2/23 Lon. R. A Coy relieved by 2nd S. LANC and 2/16 Lon. R. marched to lid.W.15 in N.15 and N.21.	
	8/11/18		In billets refitting cleaning.	

Army Form C. 2118.

WAR DIARY
or
INTELLIGENCE SUMMARY.
(Erase heading not required.)

Instructions regarding War Diaries and Intelligence Summaries are contained in F. S. Regs., Part II. and the Staff Manual respectively. Title pages will be prepared in manuscript.

Place	Date	Hour	Summary of Events and Information	Remarks and references to Appendices
Field	9/11/18		In Lillels. Coy inspected by CO in morning. Inter-Coy football in afternoon.	
	10/11/18		Bn marched to Lillers in MOEN	
	11/11/18		In Lillers. Issue of kit and checking equipment. Bn Thanksgiving Service in afternoon.	
	12/11/18		Coy parade in morning. Inter Coy football in afternoon	
	13/11/18		Football in afternoon. Concert in evening	
	14/11/18		Parades in morning. Played 2/14 Lon. R. at Rugby in afternoon. Drew 0:0	
	15/11/18		Marched to Lillers at ST ANNE	
	16/11/18		Football B:XI (0) v. REST (1) Officers (1) v. Sergts (0)	
	17/11/18		" B:XI (0) v. 98 Fld Amb: (1)	
	18/11/18		Parade. Batt. football inter coy league games.	
	19/11/18		Parade in morning. football in afternoon	
	20/11/18		Concert	
	21/11/18		Football B: z v. C Batty. 149 Bde R.F.A. 2.	
	22/11/18		Football Inter coy league games	

WAR DIARY
or
INTELLIGENCE SUMMARY.
(Erase heading not required.)

Army Form C. 2118.

Place	Date	Hour	Summary of Events and Information	Remarks and references to Appendices
	23/4/18		Football Officers & men (2) v. N.C.O. (0)	Sheet 29
	24/4/18		" Bt. (3) v. C Batty 149 Bde RFA (1)	1/40,000
	25/4/18		" Rft 2 v Sergts (1) Parades in morning	
	26/4/18		Cross country run in afternoon. Football inter reg leagues. Bde	
	27/4/18		Parade for presentation of ribbons by Div Comdr to	
	27/4/18		Parade. Cross country run. Football. Concert	
	28/4/18		2 hours route march. Bn ?	
	29/4/18		" Football Bn (3) v 2/14 Lon R (2)	Sheet 28
	30/4/18		Bde marched to LINSELLES	1/40,000

Chr. Finstein
major
Cmdg 2/16 Lon Reg

2/16th LONDON REGT.

WAR DIARY NOVEMBER 1918.
APPENDIX A

DATE	OFFICERS	O.R's	CHANGES
1-11-18	33	701	3 ORs from Hospital. 13 ORs to Hospital
2-11-18	33	691	1 OR wounded & evacuated
3-11-18	33	690	9 ORs wounded - 10 ORs evacuated to Hosp.
4-11-18	33	671	2nd Lt T.S. WHITE to England - Sick
5-11-18	32	671	1 OR wounded. 16 ORs to Hosp. 1 OR rejoined from Hospital
6-11-18	32	655	2 ORs wounded. 18 ORs to Hosp.
7-11-18	32	646	2nd Lieut HOLCOMBE M.C. to England - Sick. 1 OR to Base. 1 OR rejoined from Hospital
8-11-18	31	645	6 ORs to Hospital. England.
9-11-18	31	639	32 draft. 14 ORs from Hospital. 2 ORs to Hospital
10-11-18	31	683	20 ORs to Hospital
11-11-18	31	663	
12-11-18	31	663	
13-11-18	31	663	11 ORs from Base
14-11-18	31	674	2 ORs from Hospital. 7 ORs to Hospital
15-11-18	31	669	1 OR to Chinese Labour Corps.
16-11-18	31	668	6 ORs to Hospital England from Leave
17-11-18	31	662	Lt K FRAZER. Lt E.L. GIBBINS invalided to England. 2 ORs to Hospital. 2 ORs from Hospital
18-11-18	29	662	16 ORs from Hospital. 4 ORs draft from Base.
19-11-18	29	682	2 ORs from Hospital. 9 ORs to Hospital
20-11-18	29	675	1 OR from Hospital
21-11-18	29	676	1 OR.
22-11-18	29	677	Capt W.W. BRUCE to England. 7 ORs to Hospital. Lt Tound, Lt Steeds, 2nd Lt Kitching, 2nd Read, 2nd Lt Wood & 2nd Lt Townley
23-11-18	34	670	
24-11-18	34	670	8 ORs to Hospital
25-11-18	34	662	37 ORs from Base & Hospital
26-11-18	34	699	2nd Lt Rankin to U.K. 2 ORs from Hospital
27-11-18	33	701	32 ORs from Hospital. Capt Corlett rejoined from Hospital
28-11-18	34	733	106 ORs draft from Base. 3 ORs from Hospital
29-11-18	34	842	
30-11-18	34	842	

Index..........................

SUBJECT.

2/16th London Regt.

No.	Contents.	Date.
	December 1918.	

Secret.

Volume No 30.

War Diary
of
2/16th London Regt.
Queen's Westminster Rifles.

December 1918.

W G Pearson
Lt Col.
Commdg 2/16th London Regt.

Army Form C. 2118.

WAR DIARY
or
INTELLIGENCE SUMMARY.
(Erase heading not required.)

Vol. 30.

Instructions regarding War Diaries and Intelligence Summaries are contained in F. S. Regs., Part II. and the Staff Manual respectively. Title pages will be prepared in manuscript.

Place	Date	Hour	Summary of Events and Information	Remarks and references to Appendices
In the field	December 1st		Battn. marched from LINSELLES to LA PREVOTE.	
	2nd.		do do LA PREVOTE to LESTREM.	
	3rd.		do do LESTREM to ST. VENANT.	
	4th.		do do ST. VENANT to STEENBECQUE.	
	5th.		Bn. in billets at STEENBECQUE. Coy. inspections.	
	6th/7th		Cross country run. Bn. training.	
	8th.		Church services.	
	9th.		Boxing, training, salvage work.	
	10th to 13th		Training, salvage operations, hut construction, inter-Coy football matches, education work.	
	14th to 18th		Cross country runs, football, Baths.	
	19th to 24th.		Training, salvage operations, debates, Educational work.	
	25th		Church Services.	
	26th.		1 hrs. training parade.	

D.D. & L., London, E.C.
(A 883) Wt W807/M1672 350,000 4/17 **Sch. 52a** Forms/C/2118/14

Sheet 2.

WAR DIARY
or
INTELLIGENCE SUMMARY.

(Erase heading not required.)

Army Form C. 2118.

Place	Date	Hour	Summary of Events and Information	Remarks and references to Appendices
	December			
In the field	27th		Training, camp improvements, baths.	
	28th		do do do	
	29th		Church Services.	
	30th to		Route march, cross country run,	
	31st.		salvage operations.	

W.C.

Lieut. Col.,
Commdg. 2/16th London Regiment (C.W.R.).

2/16TH LONDON REGIMENT (Q.W.R.)

WAR DIARY, DECEMBER, 1918.

APPENDIX A.

Date	Offs	O.R.	Changes
1.12.18	34	842	
2.12.18.	34	842	
3.12.18	34	842	
4.12.18	34	842	12 O.R. to hosp
5.12.18	34	830	1 O.R. to hosp
6.12.18	34	829	2/Lt. EDWARDS, 2/Lt. CRISP, Lt. GARDINER, 2/Lt HENDERSON 2/Lt. ARNOLD from Base, 10 O.R. from hosp., 8 O.R. to hosp
7.12.18	39	831	6 O.R. to U.K. for exchange, 1 O.R. to Base, 4 O.R. to hosp., 1 O.R. from hosp.
8.12.18.	39	821	2 O.R. from hosp., 2 O.R. to Base.
9.12.18	39	821	9 O.R. from hosp
10.12.18.	39	830	2 O.R. from hosp., 1 O.R. to Base, 2 O.R. to hosp.
11.12.18	39	829	51 O.R. from hosp., 6 O.R. from Base
12.12.18	39	886	4 O.R. from hosp., 2 O.R. to demob.
13.12.18.	39	888	1 O.R. from hosp.
14.12.18	39	889	1 O.R.
15.12.18	39	890	1 O.R. to U.K. (exchange), 1 O.R. to Bde Estab., 2 O.R from hosp.
16.12.18.	39	890	2/Lt. BERNARD to U.K. (sick) 1 O.R. to base.
17.12.18	38	889	1 O.R. to demob.
18.12.18	38	888	
19.12.18	38	888	
20.12.18	38	888	
21.12.18	38	888	2 O.R. from hosp., 1 O.R. to Reserve Bn.
22.12.18	38	889	
23.12.18.	38	889	11 O.R. from hosp.
24.12.18	38	900	
25.12.18	38	900	2/Lt. POPE, Lt. TAYLOR to U.K., 3 O.R. from hosp.
26.12.18	36	903	
27.12.18	36	903	1 O.R. from hosp
28.12.18	36	904	8 O.R. to hosp,, 2 O.R. demob.
29.12.18	36	894	1 O.R. from hosp
30.12.18	36	895	1 O.R. to demob.
31.12.18	36	894	

W. Pearse
Lieut. Col.
Commdg. 2/16th London Regiment (Q.W.R.)

Army Form C. 2118.

2/16th LONDON REGIMENT.
(QUEEN'S WESTMINSTER RIFLES).

WAR DIARY
or
INTELLIGENCE SUMMARY.
(Erase heading not required.)

Instructions regarding War Diaries and Intelligence Summaries are contained in F. S. Regs., Part II. and the Staff Manual respectively. Title pages will be prepared in manuscript.

Place	Date	Hour	Summary of Events and Information	Remarks and references to Appendices
STEENBECQUE	1st Jan.		Battalion in Billets.	HAZEBROUCK.
- do -	2nd Jan.		Battn. moved by march route to DELETTE.	- do -
- do -	3 Jan.		" " from DELETTE to VERCHOUQ.	- do -
	4 "		" " VERCHOUQ to MONTCAVREL.	- do -
	5th Jan.		Battn. " MONTCAVREL to ETAPLES (LE TOUQUET).	- do -
	6th to 21st.		Battn. in camp (hutments) LE TOUQUET). Recreational Training, Educational Schemes etc. Small parties proceeded on demobilization.	CALAIS.
	22nd.		Battn. entrained ETAPLES and detrained at CALAIS (less Transport) and proceeded to No. 1 Leave Camp, BEAUMARAIS.	- do -
	23rd & 24th.		3 Coys. distributed to local depots for clerical duties and guards.	- do -
	25th to 31st.		Battn. H.Q. and 1 Coy. at No. 1 Leave Camp. Remainder as above. Daily Parties of 25 (average) proceeded to Concentration Camp for Demobilization.	- do -

Lt.Col.
2/16TH BATTALION LONDON REGIMENT
QUEEN'S WESTMINSTER RIFLES.

2/16 TH LONDON REGIMENT. (Q.W.R.)

WAR DIARY.

APPENDIX A.

1. 1. 19.	35 - 894	1 O.R.		to U.K. for demobilisation.
1. 1. 19.	35 - 893	10 O.R's		from hospital.
		7	"	to U.K. for demob.
7. 1. 19.	35 - 896	2	"	detained in U.K. whilst on leave for demob.
9. 1. 19.	35 - 894	7	"	to U.K. for demob.
		2	"	rejoined from hospital.
		26	"	evacuated to hospital.
10. 1. 19.	35 - 863	10	"	to U.K. for demob.
		22	"	rejoined from hospital.
11. 1. 19	35 - 875	21	"	to U.K. for demob.
13. 1. 19	35 - 854	3	"	rejoined from hospital.
1		13	"	to U.K. for demob.
14. 1. 19.	35 - 844	3	"	rejoined from hospital.
		9	"	to U.K. for demob.
16. 1. 19	35 - 838	4	"	rejoined from hospital.
		12	"	to hospital.
20. 1. 19	35 - 830	1	"	from hospital.
		7	"	to U.K. for demob.
22. 1. 19	35 - 824	2	"	to U.K. for demob.
24. 1. 19	35 - 822	2	"	rejoined from hospital.
25. 1. 19	35 - 824	4	"	detained in U.K. for demob.
26. 1. 19	35 - 820	1	"	from hospital.
27. 1. 19	35 - 821	4	"	from hospital.
28. 1. 19	35 - 825	6	"	to U.K. for demob.
29. 1. 19	35 - 829	57	"	to U.K. for demob.
		Lt. F.C.TICKLE granted extension of leave.		
30. 1. 19	34 - 762	28 O.R's to U.K. for demob.		
		Lt. T.J.BRUCE, M.C. to U.K. for demob.		
31. 1. 19	33 - 734	1 O.R. rejoined from hospital.		
		18 " to U.K. for demob.		
	34 - 717.			

Wey Pearson
LT. COL
O/C 2/19TH BATTALION LONDON REGIMENT.
(QUEEN'S WESTMINSTER RIFLES)

2/16th London Regiment.
(QUEEN'S WESTMINSTER RIFLES.)

Army Form C. 2118.

WAR DIARY
or
INTELLIGENCE SUMMARY.
(*Erase heading not required.*)

VOL. 33.

Instructions regarding War Diaries and Intelligence Summaries are contained in F.S. Regs., Part II. and the Staff Manual respectively. Title pages will be prepared in manuscript.

Place	Date	Hour	Summary of Events and Information	Remarks and references to Appendices
CALAIS.	1st to 28th FEB.		Battalion engaged in Guard & Clerical Duties at the following :-	CALAIS.
			No.1 Leave Camp. No.6 Leave Camp. West Quay. Fontinettes, & Vendroux	
			McCraw
Lieut. Colonel.
Commg. 2/16th London Regiment.	

2/16TH LONDON REGIMENT. (Q.W.R.)

WAR DIARY.

APPENDIX A.

	Offs.	O.R's.	
1. 2. 19	34	717	2/Lt. J.S.REEVE to U.K. for demob.
			2/Lt. W.L.PRATT to U.K. for demob.
1. 2. 19	32	666	50 O.R's to U.K. for demob.
			1 O.R. detained." " in U.K.
2. 2. 19	32	627	39 O.R's to U.K. " "
3. 2. 19	32	602	25 " " " " "
4. 2. 19	32	591	LIEUT. DE LA COUR joined from Base.
			2/Lieut. H.W.SUMSION to U.K. for demob.
			10 O.R's to U.K. for demob.
			1 O.R. transferred to 1/15th London Regt.
5. 2. 19	32	555	22 OR's to U.K. for demob.
			14 " to Hospital.
6. 2. 19	32	539	15 " to U.K. for demob.
			1 " to A.O.O. as interpreter.
7. 2. 19	32	534	4 " to U.K. for demob.
8. 2. 19	32	517	17 " - ditto -
9. 2. 19	39	614	2/Lt. H.F.WOOD to U.K. for demob.
			21 O.R's to U.K. for demob.
			Lt. A.J.N.SIEVWRIGHT, M.M. from 12th Ldns.
			Lt. B.L. JEPHSON " -do-
			2/Lt. S.J. LAMBOURNE, " -do-
			" C.C.VEITCH, " -do-
			" R. KNOX " -do-
			" H.S.SAUNDERS, M.M. " -do-
			" J.E.A.WEBSTER, M.C. " -do-
			" W.G.DAVIDSON, " -do-
			118 O.R's " -do-
10. 2. 19	38	576	Lt. G.G.STEEDS to U.K. for demob.
			32 O.R's to -do-
			6 " to Hospital.
11. 2. 19	38	552	25 " to U.K. for demob.
			1 " rejoined from Hospital.
12. 2. 19	38	537	4 " - ditto -
			19 " to U.K. for demob.
13. 2. 19	38	487	48 " - ditto -
			2 " - ditto - from Bde.
14. 2. 19	38	477	5 " - ditto -
			5 " to A.A.G., CALAIS as Clerks.
			(Auth: C.C/99/0 d/14/2/19.
15. 2. 19	38	476	1 " joined from 12th London Regt.
			2 " to U.K. for demob.
16. 2. 19	38	473	3 " - ditto - from Bde.
17. 2. 19	37	463	Lt. J.L.DE LA COUR to U.K. for demob.
			5 O.R's to U.K. for demob.
			5 " to Hospital.
20. 2. 19	37	461	2 " to U.K. for demob.
21. 2. 19	37	456	1 " - ditto -
			1 " - ditto - from Bde.
			1 " - ditto - from Div.
			2 " - ditto - from XIX Corps.
			2 " demob. whilst on leave.
			1 " rejoined from Hospital.
23. 2. 19	38	455	Lt. C.S.JEFFREY (12th Ldns) returned from leave.
24. 2. 19	37	455	Capt. & Q.M.C.J.TROLLOPE, M.C. to U.K. for demob.
26. 2. 19	37	455	1 O.R. rejoined from Hospital.
			1 " to U.K. for demob.
27. 2. 19	37	454	1 " - ditto - from Bde.
	37	454	

C.A. Rowes major
for Lt. Col.,
Commdg. 2/16th London Regt.

War Diary

of

1/16th Ln London Regt

for

February 1919

2/16th. LONDON REGIMENT.

(QUEEN'S WESTMINSTER RIFLES.)

WAR DIARY or **INTELLIGENCE SUMMARY.**

(Erase heading not required.)

Army Form C. 2118.

Vol. 33.

Vol 10

Instructions regarding War Diaries and Intelligence Summaries are contained in F. S. Regs., Part II. and the Staff Manual respectively. Title pages will be prepared in manuscript.

Place	Date	Hour	Summary of Events and Information	Remarks and references to Appendices
CALAIS.	1st. to 24th. MARCH		Battalion engaged in Guard & Clerical Duties at the following:— No.1.Leave Camp, No.6.Leave Camp, Fontinettes, & Vendroux.	CALAIS.
"	25th. to 31st. MARCH		H.Q. B. C. & D. Companies. as above.	"
	25th. to 31st. MARCH		A. Company, Guard duties at Zeneghem.	ST.OMER.

Lt.Col.
Commdg. 2/16th. London Regt.

2/16TH. LONDON REGIMENT.(Q.W.R.)
WAR DIARY.

APPENDIX A.

	Offs.	O.R's.	
1.3.19.	37	454	7 O.R's. to Hospital.
			1 O.R. rejoined from Hospital.
3.3.19.	37	448	4 O.R's. to U.K. for Demob.
			1 O.R. rejoined from Hospital.
4.3.19.	36	445	2/Lt.KERSEY to U.K. for Demob.
			3 O.R's. to U.K. for Demob.
			1 O.R. rejoined from Hospital.
5.3.19.	36	443	2/Lt.C.RANDALL. from 1/5th.London Regt.
			" H.COLES. " " " "
			" L.B.MARRIAN. " " " "
			" H.W.SNODGRASS. " " " "
			89 O.R's. " " " "
6.3.19.	40	532	1 O.R. to U.K. for Demob.
7.3.19.	40	531	Capt.Rev. G.H.WEST. to U.K. for Demob.
			2/Lt.J. ANDREWS. from 1/2nd.London Regt.
			" F.E.POWELL. " " " "
			" P.S.KEEN. " " " "
			" D.H.MARSHALL. " " " "
			" H.S.BARBER. " " " "
			69 O.R's. " " " "
8.3.19.	44	600	1 O.R. rejoined from Hospital.
			Capt.R.H.BATES. to U.K. for Demob.
11.3.19.	43	601	1 O.R. rejoined from Hospital.
12.3.19.	43	602	2 O.R's. Demob. whilst on Leave.
			2 O.R's. to U.K. Sick.
14.3.19.	43	598	2/Lt.T.H.HENDERSON. to 9th.Batt. London Regt.
			" W.B.EDWARDS. " " " " "
			" E. KITCHING. " " " " "
			" W.H.WILTSHIRE. " " " " "
			" A.H.READ. " " " " "
			" A.F.CRISP. " " " " "
			Lieut.H.G.GARDINER. " " " " "
15.3.19.	36	598	2dLt.A/Capt.T.H.SMITH. to U.K. Sick.
			2 O.R's. to U.K. for Demob.
16.3.19.	35	596	2/Lt.A/Capt.G.GRIFFITHS. to U.K. for Demob.
			2/Lt.L.C.PIERPOINT. to U.K. for Demob.
			4 O.R's. to U.K. for Demob.
18.3.19.	33	592	2/Lt. J.M.BERKELEY. from 1/5th.London Regt.
19.3.19.	34	592	1 O.R. transferred to Home Command.
22.3.19.	34	591	65 O.R's. joined from 1/34th.London Regt.
23.3.19.	34	656	7 O.R's. to Hospital.
25.3.19.	34	649	29 O.R's. joined from 1/16th.London Regt.
			36 O.R's. " " 1/13th. " "
			2/Lt. E.E.J.BLACKBURN. joined from 1/34th.Lon.RT.
			Lt.Col.R.BELLAMY D.S.O.(to replace
			" " N.G.PEARSON.D.S.O. M.C. Demob.)
			2/Lt.W.A.HARRIS, to U.K. for Demob.
26.3.19.	34	714	17 O.R's. to U.K. for Demob.
27.3.19.	34	697	
	34	697	

Lt.Col.
Commdg.2/16th.London Regt.

War Diary

of

2/16th London's Regt.

for

March 1919

2/16th. LONDON REGIMENT.
(QUEEN'S WESTMINSTER RIFLES.)

WAR DIARY
or
INTELLIGENCE SUMMARY.

VOL. 74 APRIL 1919

Vol 11

Army Form C. 2118.

Place	Date 1919	Hour	Summary of Events and Information	Remarks and references to Appendices
CALAIS	1st. to 22nd. APRIL		Battalion engaged in Guard and Clerical duties and Training at the following :-	CALAIS
"	23rd to 30th APRIL		Eton Camp, Fontinette, and Vendroux.	
"	23rd to 25th APRIL		"Q" Coy. at Fontinette for Train Guards.	CALAIS
"			"H.Q." "B" "D" and "A" Coys. at Eton Camp, Beau Marais Training.	CALAIS
"	26th to 30th APRIL		"H.Q." "B" "D" Coys. at Eton Camp Training.	CALAIS
"	26th to 30th APRIL		"A" Coy. at Vaudelievre on Ordnance Guard.	CALAIS

B. Ramsey
Lt.Col.
Commanding 2/16th. Batn. London Regt.
(Q.W.R.)

2/16th. LONDON REGIMENT (Q.W.R.)

WAR DIARY

APPENDIX A

	Offs.	O.R.s	
28.3.19	34	697	Lt. P.J.Worthington joined from 1/16th.Londons
			2/Lt. A.Farrar joined from 1/13th. Londons.
			2/Lt. W.T.Snook " " " "
			1 O.R. joined from 1/16th. London Regt.
			1 " " " 1/13th. London Regt.
			4 " s. " " 24th. London Regt.
			41 " " " 1/5 th. London Regt.
			47 " " " 1/2 nd. London Regt.
			16 O.R. " " 28th. London Regt.
			Capt.&(A/Major) C.L.Flower M.C. to U.K. for demobilisation,
			5 O.R.s. to U.K. for demobilisation.
			2/Lt. E.Cook M.M. joined from 1/24th. London Regt.
1.4.19	37	805	
2.4.19	37	805	3 O.R.s. joined from 1/24th. London Regt.
			2 O.R.s. Demobilised from Brigade.
			2/Lt. H.C.D.Eccles evacuated to U.K. sick from Hospital.
3.4.19	38	806	1 O.R. from 1/28th. London Regt.
			3 O.R.s. to U.K. for demobilisation.
4.4.19	36	804	2/Lt. F.J.Simmons from 1/16th. Londons (Detached)
			" H.J.Bugg " 1/19th. "
			" J.R.Russell " " "
			1 O.R. demobilised from Brigade.
			17 O.R.s. joined from 1/2nd. London Regt.
			6 O.R.s. " " 1/5th. " "
			3 O.R.s. " " 1/18th. " "
5.5.19.	39	829	28 O.R.s " " 1/19th. " "
			6 O.R.s " " 1/2nd " "
			6 O.R.s " " 1/16th " "
			5 O.R.s " " 1/5th " "
			26 O.R.s " " 1/13th " "
			3 O.R.s to U.K. for demob.
			2/Lt. L.J. West demob. from Bge.
7.4.19	38	894	3 O.R.s joined from 1/19th London Regt.
8.4.19	38	897	3 O.R.s " " 1/23th " "
			3 O.R.s " " 1/19th " "
			3 O.R.s " " 1/24th " "
			23 O.R.s " " 1/13th " Corps
9.4.19	38	934	1 O.R. invd. to U.K. sick from 3rd. School Eng.
			1 O.R. demob. whilst on Leave.
			2/Lt. A/Capt. G.S. Mason struck off strength & put on strength of XIX Corps.
			1 O.R. to U.K. for demob.
10.4.19	37	931	Lt.(A/Capt.) Mortimer W. to U.K. for Demobilistn.
13.4.19	36	931	4 O.R.s. Joined from 1/19th. Battn. London Regt.
			1 O.R. Re-joined from Palestine
			2 O.R.s. joined from 1/28th. London Regt.
			2/Lt. R.D.Creasey joined from 2/12th. London Regt.
			3 O.R.s. to U.K. for demobilisation.
14.4.19	37	935	38 O.R.s. joined from 1/5th. London Regt.
			18 " " " 1/16th. " "
			17 " " " 1/13th, " "
			2 " to U.K for demobilisation.
			1 O.R. taken on strength of 90th. Inf. Bde.
15.4.19	37	1005	26 O.R.s. joined from 1/2nd. London Regt.
			2/Lt. P.R.Townley to U.K. for demobilisation.
			Lieut.G.E.Found to " " "
			2 O.R.s. to " " "
16.4.19	35	1029	1 O.R. Joined from 1/19th.London Regt.
17.4.19	35	1030	12 O.R.s. " " 1/13th. B "
			1 O.R. to U.K for Demobilisation.
19.4.19	35	1041	1 O.R. Joined from 1/12th. London Regt.

	Offs.	O.R.s.	
20.4.19	35	1042	61 O.R.s. Joined from 1st. East Surrey's
			2/Lt. E.W.Dalley Joined from 1st. East Surrey's
			" P.J.McLellan " " " "
			" R.A.Stoneham " " " "
			" F.V.Jefferies " " " "
21.4.19	39	1103	" (A/Capt.) N.R.Hasluck " " "
			" J.E.Winter " " " "

52 O.R.s. Joined from 1st. East Surrey's
76 " " " 12th. K.R.R.C.
39 " " " 11th. K.R.R.C.
1 O.R. Taken on strength Twice in error.
1 O.R. " " " and put on strength of 227 D.L. & Coy.
2/Lt. F.A.Read to U.K. for Demobilisation
2 O.R.s. Struck off strength and put on strength of No. 1 Area H.Q.
1 O.R. to No. 5 Military Prison.

| 22.4.19 | 40 | 1265 | Lt. P.L.Worthington to U.K. for Demobilisation |
| 24.4.19 | 39 | 1265 | 7 O.R.s. Joined from 1/13th. London Regt. |

1 O.R. " " 1/16th. London Regt.
1 O.R. " " 1/5 th. London Regt.
2/Lt. I.J.Best to U.K for demobilisation.

| 26.4.19 | 38 | 1274 | 1 O.R. Re-joined from Hosptl. |

8 O.R.s. Struck off strength -To hospital.
5 O.R.s. " " " and put on strength of E.F.C. MONS

| 27.4.19 | 38 | 1262 | 1 O.R. Joined from East Surrey's |
| 28.4.19 | 38 | 1263 | 2 O.R.s to U.K for demobilisation. |

2/Lt. J.S.Arnold to U.K for demobilisation.
Lt. C.J.Jeffrey " " "
2/Lt. G.R.Bussell " " "
" E.B.Blackburn " " "

| 29.4.19 | 34 | 1261 | 2 O.R.s. to U.K. for demobilisation. |

3 O.R.s. to U.K. Sick

| 30.4.19 | 34 | 1256 | 2/Lt. J.Andrews to U.K. for demobilisation |

2 O.R.s. Transferred to Home establishment.
1 O.R. Invalided to U.K.

| | 33 | 1253 | |

War Diary

of

//16th London Regt.

for

April 1919

SECRET.

WAR DAIRY

OF THE

2/16TH. LONDON REGIMENT,

(QUEEN'S WESTMINSTER RIFLES.)

FOR THE MONTH OF

MAY, 1919.

ABBEVILLE,
5-6-19.

2/16th. LONDON REGIMENT.
(QUEEN'S WESTMINSTER RIFLES)
WAR DIARY
or
INTELLIGENCE SUMMARY.   VOL. 35 MAY 1919.
(Erase heading not required.)

Army Form C. 2118.

Place	Date	Hour	Summary of Events and Information	Remarks and references to Appendices
	1919.			
CALAIS	1st. to 28th. MAY.		'HQ' 'B' & 'D' Coys. at Eton Camp Training & furnishing Ordnance & A.S.C. Guard Duties.	CALAIS
"	1st. to 5th. MAY		'A' Coy. at Valdelièvre on Ordnance Guard.	"
"	6th. to 28th. MAY		'A' Coy. at RINXENT furnishing P.O.W. Guards.	"
"	1st. to 27th. MAY		'C' Coy. at FONTINETTES for Train Guards.	"
"	28th. to 29th. MAY		Battalion concentrated at Eton Camp BEAUMARAIS for move to ABBEVILLE.	"
"	30th MAY		Battalion and Transport moved by rail from FONTINETTES to ABBEVILLE. Accomodated at Signal Depot.	ABBEVILLE
"	31st MAY		'A' Coy. to FOCH CAMP ABBEVILLE for duty (1 Platoon detached to E.F.C. NOYELLES)	
			'B' Coy. Ammunition Dump DIEVAL, Guard duties.	DIEVAL.
			'C' Coy. No. 2 P.O.W. Cage as P.O.W. Guards.	ABBEVILLE
			'D' Coy. 24 Ordnance Dump DOMLEGAR as Guard duties.	DOMLEGAR
			'HQ' & 'Tpt.' at Signal Depot.	ABBEVILLE

Lieut. Colonel,
Commanding 2/16th. LONDON REGIMENT (Q.W.R.)

2/16th. LONDON REGIMENT.
(QUEEN'S WESTMINSTER RIFLES.)

WAR DIARY

APPENDIX 'A'

Date.	Offs.	O.R.s.	
1/5/19	33	1253	2 O.R.s joined from 1/16th. London Regt.
			7 O.R.s to U.K. for re-enlistment Furlough
2/5/19	33	1248	1 O.R. joined from 12th. K.R.R.C.
			3 O.R.s to U.K. for re-enlistment Furlough
3/5/19	33	1246	5 O.R.s joined from 1/5th. Londons (Detached)
			1 O.R. " " 1/16th. " "
			2 O.R.s. " " 1/2nd. " "
			1 O.R. " " 1/13th. " "
			4 O.R.s, " " 1/19th. " "
6/5/19	33	1259	2 O.R.s to U.K. for Re-enlistment Furlough
			1 O.R. to Hspital.
7/5/19	33	1256	2/Lieut. Van Coller joined from 1/28th. London Regt.
			2 O.R.s. taken on strength twice in error
			8 O.R.s. to Hospital.
8/5/19	34	1246	1 O.R. to U.K. for Demobilization.
10/5/19	34	1245	3 O.R.s. joined from 1/28th. London Regt.
			1 O.R. " " 1/19th. " "
12/5/19	34	1249	1 O.R. posted to 1/13th. London Regt.
			(Auth.56 Div.AQ.X.1500/348.)
14/5/19	34	1248	1 O.R. joined from Hspital
			1 O.R. " " 1/28th. London Regt.
16/5/19	34	1250	11 O.R.s joined from 11th. K.R.R.C.
			1 O.R. Joined from Hospital.
			4 O.R.s. to U.K. for Demobilization.
18/5/19	34	1258	1 O.R. joined from 1/5th. Londons (Detached)
21/5/19	34	1259	1 O.R. joined from Hospital.
			2/Lieut. C.E.Winter Demobilized Gp.45b.
			1 O.R. tp U.K. for Demobilization.
23/5/19	33	1259	1 O.R. joined from 11th. K.R.R.C.
24/5/19	33	1260	R.S.M. Carroll joined from 2nd. Scottish Rifles Havre B.D.
25/5/19	33	1261	1 O.R. demobilized whilst on leave.
26/5/19	33	1260	1 O.R. joined from Hospital.
			13 O.R.s. to Hospital.
27/5/19	33	1248	1 O.R. Joined from Hospital.
			1 O.R. to U.K. for demobilization.
28/5/19	33	1248	

SECRET.

WAR DIARY

OF

2/16TH. LONDON REGIMENT.
(QUEEN'S WESTMINSTER RIFLES)

FOR THE MONTH OF

JUNE, 1919.

(VOLUME NO. 36)

ABBEVILLE
3/7/19.

LIEUT. COL.
Commanding 2/16th. LONDON REGT. (Q.W.R.)

Army Form C. 2118.

2/16th LONDON REGIMENT
(QUEEN'S WESTMINSTER RIFLES.)

WAR DIARY
or
INTELLIGENCE SUMMARY.
(Erase heading not required.)

VOL.36

JUNE 1919.

Place	Date	Hour	Summary of Events and Information	Remarks and references to Appendices
ABBEVILLE.	1919. JUNE. 4th.		Battn. H.Qs. Tpt. "B" & "D" Coy. Details moved from Signal Depot to No. 5 Vet. Camp.	ABBEVILLE
	13th.		"D" Coy. Detachment to No. 23 Vehicle Reception Camp Park furnishing Guards.	"
	23rd.		"B". Coy. Detachment of 25 O.Rs. to A.P.M. ABBEVILLE for attachment to M.F.P.	"
	1st. to 30th.		"A" Coy. at Foch Camp furnishing P.O.W. Guards, and Training (2 Platoons) 1 Platoon at NOYELLES attached E.F.C.	"
	1st. to 30th.		"B" Coy. 2 Platoons at DIEVAL furnishing Dump Guards. 12 O.R. Detachment furnishing Guard, Detention Compound. Details with Bn. H.Q. No. 5 Vet. Camp.	DIEVAL. ABBEVILLE
	1st. to 30th.		"C" Coy. at No. 2 P.O.W. Main Cage furnishing P.O.W. Escorts and Guards	"
	1st. to 30th.		"D" Coy. at DOMLEGER furnishing Ammunition Dump Guards.	DOMLEGER

Lieut. Colonel,
Commanding 2/16th. LONDON REGIMENT (Q.W.R.)

2/16th. LONDON REGIMENT.
(QUEEN'S WESTMINSTER RIFLES.)

WAR DIARY.

APPENDIX 'A'.

Date			
1-6-1919	33	1248	1 O.R. joined from 34th. Londons.
			1 O.R. joined from Hospital.
			1 O.R. transferred to M.F.P.
1-6-1919	33	1249	2/Lieut. C.D.Smith to Russian Relief Force.
			1 O.R. joined from 1/16th. Londons.
2-6-1919	32	1250	Lieut. L.P.B.Doman joined from Som.L.I.
			1 O.R. to Home Command.
5-6-1919	33	1249	1 O.R. from Hospital.
7-6-1919	33	1250	2 O.Rs. posted from 1/13th. Londons.
			1 O.R. posted from 1/16th. Londons.
			1 O.R. posted from 1/5th. Londons.
8-6-1919	33	1254	5 O.Rs. to Hospital.
9-6-1919	33	1249	1 O.R. to U.K. for Demobilization
			2/Lieut. F.S.Simonds to U.K. for Demob.
			1 O.R. transferred to 2/23rd. London Regt.
13-6-1919	32	1247	1 O.R. joined from Hospital.
			1 O.R. taken off strength. Taken on strength in duplicate.
14-6-1919	32	1247	1 O.R. transferred to Home Command
			3 O.Rs. to U.K. for Demobilization.
15-6-1919	32	1243	2/Lieut. E.Cook to U.K. for demobilization.
	31	1243	1 O.R. joined from Hospital.
			13 O.Rs. to Hospital.
			1 O.R. transferred to D.A.P.S.BOULOGNE.
17-6-1919	31	1230	1 O.R. joined from Hospital.
			1 O.R. to U.K. for demobilization.
18-6-1919	31	1230	1 O.R. to D.A.P.S. BOULOGNE.
			30 O.Rs. transferred to R.A.S.C. CALAIS.
20-6-1919	31	1199	1 O.R. transferred to R.A.S.C. CALAIS.
23-6-1919	31	1198	1 O.R. joined from Hospital.
			1 O.R. to U.K. for demobilization.
24-6-1919	31	1198	2/Lieut. W.T.Snook to U.K. for Demob.
			23 O.Rs. to C.L.C. NOYELLES.
			2 O.Rs. D.A.P.S BOULOGNE.
25-6-1919	30	1173	2 O.Rs. joined from 1/2nd. Londons.
			8 O.Rs. to ETAPLES Pool of Clerks.
			3 O.Rs. to U.K. for Demobilization.
			1 O.R. to U.K. for "
26-6-1919	30	1163	5 O.Rs. to Pool of Clerks ETAPLES.
27-6-1919	30	1158	1 O.R. to U.K. for Demobilization.
	30	1157	

Lieut. Colonel,
Commanding 2/16th. LONDON REGIMENT,
(Q.W.R.)

SECRET.

WAR DIARY.
****

O F

2/16th. LONDON REGIMENT.
(QUEEN'S WESTMINSTER RIFLES.)

FOR THE MONTH OF J U L Y 1919.

(VOL. No. 36)

Lieut. Colonel,
Commanding 2/16th. Bn. LONDON REGIMENT,
(Q.W.R.)

ABBEVILLE.

Army Form C. 2118.

2/16th. LONDON REGIMENT.
(QUEEN'S WESTMINSTER RIFLES.)

WAR DIARY
or
INTELLIGENCE SUMMARY.

VOL. 36   JULY 1919.

(*Erase heading not required.*)

Place	Date	Hour	Summary of Events and Information	Remarks and references to Appendices
ABBEVILLE.	1919. JULY 1st. to 31st.		Bn. Headquarters, Transport, 'B' Company Details, at No. 5 Vety. Camp.	ABBEVILLE.
	1st. to 31st.		'A' Company (1½ Platoons) at Foch Camp furnishing P.O.W. Guards & Training. One Platoon at NOYELLES attached to E.F.C.	NOYELLES.
	22nd. to 31st.		'A' Company 1½ Platoons at No. 2 A.S.D. MAUTORT, supplying Guards and Picquets.	MAUTORT
	1st. to 31st.		'B' Company 2 Platoons at DIEVAL furnishing Dump Guards. 14 O.R. Detachment furnishing Guards. Detention Compound. 25 O.R. Detachment attached A.P.M. ABBEVILLE.	DIEVAL. ABBEVILLE.
	1st. to 31st.		'C' Company at No. 2 P.O.W. Main Cage furnishing P.O.W. Escorts & Guards.	ABBEVILLE
	1st. to 31st.		'D' Company (3 Platoons) at DOMLEGER furnishing Dump Guards. (1 Platoon) at No. 23 V.R.P. ABBEVILLE, furnishing Guards.	DOMLEGER. ABBEVILLE.

Lieut. Colonel,
Commanding 2/16th. LONDON REGIMENT,
(Q.W.R.)

2/16th. LONDON REGIMENT.
(QUEEN'S WESTMINSTER RIFLES.)

W A R D I A R Y.

APPENDIX A. JULY 1919.

Date			
1-7-1919	30	1157	1 O.R. joined from 1/28th. Londons.
			1 O.R. joined from 56th. Div. Details.
			2 O.Rs. joined from Hospital
			1 O.R. to U.K. for Demobilization.
			1 O.R. transferred to A.P.S.
			1 O.R. transferred to Pool of Clerks ETAPLES
			25 O.Rs. to Hospital.
2-7-1919	30	1133	1 O.R. joined from 1/2nd. Londons.
			1 O.R. joined from Hospital.
			Lt. & Q.M. E.W.N. Jackson from 1/16th. Londons
			1 O.R. to U.K. for Demobilization.
3-7-19	31	1134	2 O.Rs. from Hospital
			1 O.R. from 1/2nd. London Regiment.
5-7-19	31	1137	5 O.Rs. from Hospital
			14 O.Rs. transferred to 2/14th. Londons.
6-7-19	31	1128	1 O.R. from Hospital.
9-7-19	31	1129	2 O.Rs. from Hospital
10-7-19	31	1131	1 O.R. from Hospital
11-7-19	31	1132	52 O.Rs. transferred to P.O.W. Coy. ABBEVILLE.
12-7-19	31	1080	6 O.Rs. transferred D.A.P.S. BOULOGNE.
13-7-19	31	1074	1 O.R. from 1/23rd. London Regiment.
14-7-19	31	1075	2 O.Rs. from Hospital.
15-7-19	31	1077	2 O.Rs. to U.K. for R/E Leave
16-7-19	31	1075	1 O.R. to U.K. for demobilization.
18-7-19	31	1074	1 O.R. from Hospital.
			3 O.Rs. from 2/14th. London Regiment.
19-7-19	31	1078	1 O.R. from Hospital.
21-7-19	31	1079	1 O.R. S/O Strength admitted to Hospital whilst on U.K. leave.
			1 O.R. transferred to 52nd. Bedford Regiment.
			1 O.R. transferred to 9th. Bn. East Surrey's.
23-7-29	31	1076	3 O.Rs. from Hospital
			2 O.Rs. to R.A.O.C. CALAIS.
			24 O.Rs. to Hospital.
			1 O.R. transferred to Home Command from leave
24-7-19	31	1052	2 O.Rs. to U.K. for R/E Leave.
			2 O.Rs. from Hospital.
26-7-19	31	1052	8 O.Rs. transferred to C.O.O. CALAIS.
			1 O.R. transferred H.M. Prison ROUEN.
			1 O.R. from Hospital.
27-7-19	31	1044	2 O.Rs. transferred to R.A.S.C. (M.T.).
29-7-19	31	1042	3 O.Rs. from Hospital.
	31	1045.	

SECRET.
****

WAR DIARY

OF

2/16th. BATTALION THE LONDON REGIMENT.
(QUEEN'S WESTMINSTER RIFLES.)

FOR THE MONTH OF

AUGUST 1919.

VOL. NO. 37.

ABBEVILLE.

AUGUST 30 th. 1919.

Lieutenant-Col.
COMMANDING 2/16th. BATTN. THE LONDON REGIMENT.(Q.W.R.)

Army Form C. 2118.

2/16th. LONDON REGIMENT
(QUEEN'S WESTMINSTER RIFLES.)

WAR DIARY
or
INTELLIGENCE SUMMARY.

VOLUME 37.   AUGUST 1919.

(Erase heading not required.)

Instructions regarding War Diaries and Intelligence Summaries are contained in F. S. Regs., Part II. and the Staff Manual respectively. Title pages will be prepared in manuscript.

Place	Date	Hour	Summary of Events and Information	Remarks and references to Appendices
ABBEVILLE.	1919 AUGUST 1st. to 31st.		Battn. Headquarters, Transport and 'B' Coy. at No.5 Vety. Camp.	ABBEVILLE.
	1st. to 31st.		'A' Coy. (1½ Platoons) at Foch Camp furnishing P.O.W. Guards and Training.	ABBEVILLE.
			One Platoon at NOYELLES attached to E.F.C.	NOYELLES.
			1½ Platoons at MAUTORT No.2 A.S.D. supplying guards and Picquets.	MAUTORT.
	1st. to 31st.		'B' Coy. 2 Platoons at DIEVAL furnishing dump guards.	DIEVAL.
			25 O.Rs. Detachment attached A.P.M. ABBEVILLE.	ABBEVILLE.
			14 O.Rs. Detachment furnishing guards Detention Compound.	"
	15th to 31st		10 O.Rs. Detachment LIGNY ST. FLOCHEL furnishing guards.	LIGNY ST. FLOCHEL
	1st. to 31st.		'C' Coy. at No.2 , P.O.W. Coy. Main Cage furnishing P.O.W. Escorts & Guards.	ABBEVILLE.
	1st. to 31st.		'D' Coy. 3 Platoons at DOMLEGER furnishing Dump Guards.	DOMLEGER.
			1 Platoon at No.23 V.R.P. ABBEVILLE furnishing Guards.	ABBEVILLE.

Lieutenant-Colonel,
Commanding 2/16th. London Regiment (Q.W.R.)

2/16th. LONDON REGIMENT.
(QUEEN'S WESTMINSTER RIFLES.)

WAR DIARY.

APPENDIX A. AUGUST 1919.

Date			
1-8-1919	31	1045	1 O.R. to U.K. for R.E. furlough.
			1 O.R. from Hospital.
			1 O.R. transferred to 90th. Brigade Estab.
2-8-1919	31	1044	1 O.R. from 1/28th. London Regiment.
3-8-1919	31	1045	1 O.R. transferred to Home Estab.
			1 O.R. from Hospital.
7-8-1919	31	1045	1 O.R. from Hospital.
			3 O.Rs. transferred to Truck Kitchen Bn. CALAIS.
			2 O.Rs. transfered to D.O.R.E. CAMIERS.
8-8-1919	31	1041	1 O.R. from Hospital.
			3 O.Rs. to U.K. for R.E. furlough.
9-8-1919	31	1039	1 O.R. from 1/12th. London Regiment.
			1 O.R. from Hospital.
10-8-1919	31	1041	19 O.Rs. to Hospital
			Lieut. R.G.L.Shuter to Hospital.
11-8-1919	30	1022	1 O.R. from Hospital.
13-8-1919	30	1023	1 O.R. from Hospital.
			1 O.R. from Hospital.
			2/Lieut. H.S.Chester joined from 2/17th.Lon. Regt.
15-8-1919	31	1025	5 O.Rs. from Hospital.
			1 O.R. from 1/2nd. London Regiment.
			1 O.R. s/o strength transferred to Sub-area Commandant BETHUNE.
			1 O.R. from Hospital.
16-8-1919	31	1030	2 O.Rs. from Hospital.
			1 O.R. to U.K. for demobilization. (Z56)
			1 O.R. from 1/20th. London Regiment.
			1 O.R. from 11th. K.R.R.C.
18-8-1919	31	1033	2 O.Rs. from Hospital.
			1 O.R. from 8th. London Regiment.
19-8-1919	31	1036	1 O.R. from Hospital.
			1 O.R. to U.K. for R.E. furlough.
20-8-1919	31	1036	2 O.Rs. from Hospital.
			1 O.R. from 2/20th. London Regiment.
			1 O.R. from 1/33rd. London Regiment.
23-8-1919	31	1040	3 O.Rs. s/o strength to Sch. of Cookery AUBENGUE.
			1 O.R. from Records, London as deserter.
24-8-1919	31	1038	1 O.R. s/o Strength, deserter, (Rfn. Blackwell)
26-8-1919	31	1037	5 O.Rs. to U.K. for Demobilization.
27-8-1919	31	1032	1 O.R. joined from 56th. Divnl. Details.
28-8-1919	31	1033	64 O.Rs. to U.K. for Demobilization.
			3 O.Rs. transferred to R.E. Signals.
29-8-1919	31	966	61 O.Rs. to U.K. for Demobilization.
			1 O.R. from Hospital.
30-8-1919	31	906	10 O.Rs. to U.K. for Demobilization.
			1 O.R. from Brigade taken on strength.
			1 O.R. taken on srength twice in error.
			1 O.R. from Hospital.
31-8-1919	31	897	

SECRET.

> HEADQUARTERS.
> ABBEVILLE AREA.
> No 73/B
> Date 3.10.19

WAR DIARY

OF

2/16th. LONDON REGIMENT,
(QUEEN'S WESTMINSTER RIFLES.)

FOR THE MONTH OF

SEPTEMBER 1919.

(VOLUME NO. 38.)

ABBEVILLE.
OCTOBER 2nd. 1919.

[signature]
MAJOR.
COMMANDING 2/16th. LONDON REGIMENT.(Q. W. R.)

Army Form C. 2118.

WAR DIARY
or
INTELLIGENCE SUMMARY.

2/16th. LONDON REGIMENT—
(QUEEN'S WESTMINSTER RIFLES)
VOLUME 38.   SEPTEMBER 1919.

(Erase heading not required.)

Instructions regarding War Diaries and Intelligence Summaries are contained in F. S. Regs., Part II. and the Staff Manual respectively. Title pages will be prepared in manuscript.

Place	Date SEPTEMBER 1919.	Hour	Summary of Events and Information	Remarks and references to Appendices
ABBEVILLE	1st. to 30th.		Battn. H.Q., Transport & 'B' Coy. HQ at No.5 Veterinary Camp.	ABBEVILLE
	25th. to 30th.		'A' 'B' 'C' & 'D' Coys. concentrated at No. 5 Vety. Camp to complete Demobilization and re-posting of retainable personnel.	-do-
	1st. to 24th.		'A' Coy. 1½ Platoons at Foch Camp furnishing P.O.W. Guards.	-do-
	1st. to 25th.		'A' Coy. 1 Platoon at NOYELLES attached to E.F.C.	NOYELLES.
	1st. to 24th.		'A' Coy. 1½ Platoons at MAUTORT supplying Guards and Picquets.	MAUTORT.
	1st. to 23rd.		'B' Coy. 2 Platoons at DIEVAL supplying Dump Guards.	DIEVAL.
	1st. to 24th.		25 O.Rs. attached A.P.M. ABBEVILLE.	ABBEVILLE.
	1st. to 24th.		14 O.Rs. Detachment furnishing Guard at Detention Compound.	-do-
	1st. to 18th.		'C' Coy. at No.2 P.O.W. Coy., Main Cage furnishing P.O.W. Escorts and Guards.	-do-
	1st. to 21st.		'D' Coy. 5 Platoons at Domleger furnishing Dump Guards.	DOMLEGER.
			1 Platoon at 23 V.R.P. ABBEVILLE furnishing Guards.	ABBEVILLE.

Major,
Commanding 2/16th. LONDON REGIMENT. (Q.W.R.)

2/16th. LONDON REGIMENT.
(QUEEN'S WESTMINSTER RIFLES)

WAR DIARY.

APPENDIX 'A'.   SEPTEMBER 1919.

	Offs.	O.Rs.	
1-9-1919.	31	897	1 O.R. from P.O.W. Camp, HAVRE.
			2 O.Rs. to U.K. for Demobilization.
			2 O.Rs. transferred to R.A.S.C.
2-9-1919.	31	894	1 O.R. from Hospital.
			12 O.Rs. to U.K. for Demobilization.
4-9-1919.	31	883	3 O.Rs. " " "
			1 O.R. from Hospital.
5-9-1919.	31	881	1 O.R. from D.A.P.S., BOULOGNE.
			1 O.R. from Hospital.
6-9-1919.	31	883	8 O.Rs. to U.K. for Demobilization.
7-9-1919.	31	875	Lieut. R.G.L.Shuter from Hospital.
			12 O.Rs. to U.K. for Demobilization.
8-9-1919.	32	863	10 " " "
12-9-1919.	32	853	2 O.Rs. from Hospital.
			1 O.R. to R.E.Signals.
13-9-1919.	32	854	5 O.Rs. to U.K. for Demobilization.
14-9-1919.	32	849	3 O.Rs. " "
15-9-1919.	32	846	1 O.R. from Hospital.

2/Lieut. H.S.Barber
" R.D.Creasey
Lieut. P.J.McLellan
2/Lieut. W.N.L.Stoneham   To U.K. for
" H.S.Saunders M.M.   Demobilization.
Lieut. A.Farrar
2/Lieut. F.E.Powell

17-9-1919.	25	847	33 O.Rs. to U.K. for Demobilization.
18-9-1919.	25	814	30 O.Rs. " " "
19-9-1919.	25	784	29 O.Rs. " " "
20-9-1919.	25	755	27 O.Rs. " " "
21-9-1919.	25	728	35 O.Rs. " " "
			Capt. N.R.Hasluck to U.K. for Demobilization.
22-9-1919.	24	693	22 O.Rs. to U.K. for Demobilization.
			1 O.R. from Hospital.
23-9-1919.	24	672	62 O.Rs. to U.K. for Demobilization.
			1 O.R. from Hospital.
24-9-1919.	24	611	57 O.Rs. to Leave & transferred to 16th. K.R.R.C.
			3 O.Rs. from R.E. Signals.
25-9-1919.	24	557	53 O.R. to U.K. for Demobilization.
			78 O.Rs. to Leave & transferred to 16th. K.R.R.C.
26-9-1919.	24	426	51 O.Rs. to U.K. for Demobilization.
			4 O.Rs. transferred to A.D.P.S. DIEPPE.
27-9-1919.	24	371	2/Lt. P.S.Keen to War Office as Educational Instructor.
28-9-1919.	23	371	35 O.Rs. to Leave & transferred to 16th.K.R.R.C.
			17 O.Rs. to U.K. for Demobilization.
			11 O.Rs. transferred to A.D.P.S., DIEPPE.
29-9-1919.	23	308	38 O.Rs. to U.K. for Demobilization.
			3 O.Rs. returned from Demob. Concen. Camp.
			1 O.R. from Hospital.
30-9-1919	23	274	

SECRET

WAR DIARY

OF

2/16th. LONDON REGIMENT.
(QUEEN'S WESTMINSTER RIFLES.)

for the month of

OCTOBER 1919

(VOLUME No 39).

signature
Captain.
Commanding 2/16th. LONDON REGIMENT.
(Q.W.R.).

ABBEVILLE.

(6414) Wt. W3906/P1607 2,500,000 7/18 McA & W Ltd (E 3591) Forms W3091/4.   Army Form W.3091.

Cover for Documents.

Nature of Enclosures.

Notes, or Letters written.

Army Form C. 2118.

WAR DIARY
or
INTELLIGENCE SUMMARY.

(Erase heading not required.)

2/16th. LONDON REGIMENT.
(QUEEN'S WESTMINSTER RIFLES.)
VOLUME 39. OCTOBER 1919.

Place	Date	Hour	Summary of Events and Information	Remarks and references to Appendices
ABBEVILLE	OCTOBER 1919. 1st. to 31st.		Details Company at No. 5. Veterinary Camp for purpose of Demobilisation and the re-posting of retainable personnel.	ABBEVILLE.

[signature]
Captain.
Commanding 2/16th. LONDON REGIMENT.
(Q.W.R.).

2/16th. LONDON REGIMENT.
(QUEEN'S WESTMINSTER RIFLES.)

W A R   D I A R Y

APPENDIX 'A'   OCTOBER 1919

	Offs.	O.Rs.	
1-10-19.	23	274	4 O.Rs. to U.K. for Demobilisation.
2-10-19.	23	270	1 O.R. to Hospital.
3-10-19.	23	269	7 O.Rs. to Hospital.
			5 O.Rs. to U.K. for Demobilisation.
			1 O.R. posted to M.M.P.
4-10-19.	23	256	3 O.Rs. to Arras Sub-Area.
			1 O.R. to Hospital.
			1 O.R. to A.P.M. 10th. Corps Rhine Army.
5-10-19.	23	251	
6-10-19.	23	251	1 O.R. from Hospital.
7-10-19.	23	252	
8-10-19.	23	252	
9-10-19.	23	252	
10-10-19.	23	252	
11-10-19.	23	252	1 O.R. from Hospital.
12-10-19.	23	253	42 O.Rs. to U.K. for Demobilisation
			Major. H.D.Corlett to U.K. for Demobilisation
			40 O.Rs. posted to 16th. Bn. K.R.R.C.
13-10-19.	22	171	6 O.Rs. to U.K. for Demobilisation.
14-10-19.	22	165	56 Detached O.Rs. S/O Strength.
15-10-19.	22	109	1 O.R. from Prison.
			3 O.Rs. to U.K. for Demobilisation.
16-10-19.	22	107	2 O.Rs. to U.K. for Demobilisation.
			1 O.R. to D.A.P.M. Abbeville.
17-10-19.	22	104	36 O.Rs. posted to 16th. Bn. K.R.R.C.
			2 O.Rs. to U.K. for Demobilisation.
18-10-19.	22	66	1 O.R. to U.K. for Demobilisation.
19-10-19.	22	65	
20-10-19.	22	65	3 O.Rs. to U.K. for Demobilisation.
21-10-19.	22	62	1 O.R. to U.K. for Demobilisation.
22-10-19.	22	61	5 O.Rs. to U.K. for Demobilisation.
			15 O.Rs. posted to 16th. Bn. K.R.R.C.
			Lieut. J.E.A.Webster M.C. to 119 Labour Exhumation Coy.
			Lieut. J.M.Berkley to 119 Labour Exhumation Coy.
23-10-19	20	43	Lieut. A.J.N.Sievwright to U.K. for Demob.
			Lieut. B.L.Jephson to U.K. for Demob.
			Lieut. H.G.Bugg to U.K. for Demob.
			Lieut. R.H.L.Shuter to U.K. for Demob.
			2/Lt. H.S.Chester to U.K. for Demob.
			2/Lt. E.W.Dalley to U.K. for Demob.
			4 O.Rs. to Hospital.
24-10-19	14	39	1 O.R. to U.K. for Demobilisation.
			2/Lt. L.Van Coller to U.K. for Demob.
			2/Lt. H.W.Snodgrass to U.K. for Demob.
			1 O.R. to H.Qs. Abbeville Sub-District.

APPENDIX 'A' Continued.

	Offs.	O.Rs.	
25-10-19.	12	37	2/Lt. F.V.Jeffries to U.K. for Demob.
			2/Lt. R.Knox to U.K. for Demob.
			2/Lt. C.C.Veitch to U.K. for Demob.
			Lieut. C.Randall to U.K. for Demob.
			Lieut. L.P.B.Doman to 708 Labour Exhumation Company.
			9 O.Rs. posted to 16th. Bn. K.R.R.C.
			Lieut. Col., R.Bellamy D.S.O. C. of I.
			Paris S/O of Strength
			1 O.R. from Hospital.
26-10-19.	6	29	2 O.Rs. to U.K. for Demobilisation.
27-10-19.	6	27	
28-10-19.	6	27	2/Lt L.B.Marriam to U.K. for Demob.
			1 O.R. to U.K. for Demob.
			2/Lt S.J.Lambourne to 119 Labour Exhumation Company.
29-10-19.	4	26	2 O.Rs. to 19 Labour Group, Abbeville
30-10-19.	4	24	
31-10-19.	4	24	

(signature) Captain

2/16TH BATTALION LONDON REGIMENT
(QUEEN'S WESTMINSTER RIFLES.)

www.ingramcontent.com/pod-product-compliance
Lightning Source LLC
Chambersburg PA
CBHW081445160426
43193CB00013B/2394